A CONVERSATION ABOUT THE GOOD OLD DAYS

I REMEMBER WHEN

Doris C. Smith

authorHOUSE®

AuthorHouse™
1663 Liberty Drive
Bloomington, IN 47403
www.authorhouse.com
Phone: 833-262-8899

Published by AuthorHouse 09/15/2021

ISBN: 978-1-6655-3810-7 (sc)
ISBN: 978-1-6655-3820-6 (e)

As a child, I really didn't have a relationship with my Father. As a matter of fact, I didn't care for him very much, because I thought he was so mean. It wasn't until I was grown that I found out "who" my Father "really" was. I made many judgments that was not accurate and many things I had to ask the Lord for forgiveness. I had to realize that He wasn't a "perfect man" but He was the Father that was given to me.

I saw my Mother go through many things with him. I couldn't understand and sometimes wondered, WHY? Now, I can see her strength. Today I'm grateful because she's still teaching me, how to be strong. Even thought she's deceased, some days I can STILL hear her voice.

Years later,

I was sitting and talking with my Father about his life. He shared many things. I found out that he wasn't this "boogie man" that Satan displayed in my head. So many stories he shared and they were good, as well as funny.

I've shared some of them with you.

Now, You share them with your Family.

I often say, "Leave a Legacy!"

I HOPE YOU ENJOY THE CONVERSATION!

Dedication

To God,

Who made all of this Possible

In memory of my Father,

Sergeant Ozell Conley,

Who allowed me to write His story

In memory of my Lovely Mother,

Ora Bell Conley

In memory of my Grandparents

Special Thanks

To my Children

To my Grandchildren

Also, in memory of

Sergeant Mario T. Welch

Contents

The "Chicken" Story

I remember the time when my Brother killed Mama's chickens. My Sister knew he did it and told Mama. She would be the one to "carry" the news, you know.

She knew if she didn't tell it, She'd get a whipping too. She said, "Mama, I'll tell you where your chickens are, if you don't let him whip me!"

So, Mama found out where the chickens were and "pretended" to still be looking for them.

She would call them, "Here chick, chick!" "Here chick, chick!"

He had took the chickens, strained them on a cane, and hid them behind the garden.

Putting the chickens behind the garden was just "badness." He would catch them "off the yard" because he was mischievous.

Sometimes, he would pick one and turn him a loose, ALIVE!

He would do these things and know he was going to get a whipping. He would "still" do it though.

Mama had so many chickens. Sometimes, she'd miss them and sometimes, she wouldn't.

That's where he got the name "Chicken" from.

Another time he was smoking....

That's where the chickens conversation came up. That's how the "Chicken Hunt" started.

He would take the chicken, and go to the store. He would
sell the chickens and buy some smoking tobacco.

People would take a "fryer chicken" and you would
get pretty good money for them.

He would buy tobacco, candy, and other "what not things."

Some of my Cousins was out there smoking but
wouldn't let my younger Cousin go.

Mama asked, "Why y'all keep running out there to the barn?"

My little Cousin, mad because they wouldn't let him smoke said,
"I'll tell you what they are doing; they out there smoking!"

Mama said, What! They out there smoking...

My Cousin said, "They sold a chicken at the store."

So, when my Brother came back, Mama searched him, you know!

That scoundrel was pretty smart. He had it tied on the end of his
shirt-tail and hanging down his "britches" but Mama found it.

She said, "Uh Huh, I am going to carry this and give it to your Daddy!"
I ain't going to bother you, I'm going to let your Daddy handle this!"

So, that night, we sat around the fire. I sat and sat, my Brother sat
and sat. Mama went on to bed. Papa went to sleep in the chair. We
knew what was going to happen. So, we tried to "out-set" Papa.

We thought He'd go to bed but HE DIDN'T.

Mama made us get up and go to bed. I said, "Lord, we're in big trouble now!"

So, when we went to bed, my Brother went to sleep, but I
didn't because I knew what was going to happen.

Later,

Papa came in there, and Lord, He "tore" my Brother up. He did! He made Him tell where He got that tobacco.

When Papa went to go out of the room, I jumped up, got out of the bed and got behind the door. I was "scared to death."

When He went out, He was pulling the door up; He wasn't going to bother me, but "me being scared" I said, "Oh Papa, I didn't do it!"

I liked to fainted! I just threw up both hands, "Oh Papa, I didn't do it!"

Papa said, "Come from back there and go to bed!" I was scared to death!

I'd been in some of the smoking but I wasn't with them that time. If I had of been with them, I would have gotten it too.

Children didn't get away with too much back then. Parents would tell you something "one time." The next time, you got a whipping.

Now, my Daddy, if you told Him the truth, you'd probably wouldn't get a whipping. But...Sometimes, he would though.

But if you told a lie, you'd get two whippings. He would whip you until you tell the truth and then whip you for lying.

Visiting My Grandparents

When I'd go to my Grandparents house, I'd ask to stay with my Uncle.

I loved staying with him because He liked "caring on a lot of fun."

When I would ask him about going home with him, He
would say, "Wait Son, until I ask; don't be putting yourself
off on nobody!" But, he would only be joking.

He was always real funny, you know!

My Granddaddy had an old dog there. This dog had more sense
than "anything you ever seen." If he saw anyone around the
house, that dog would search to see who and what they were
doing there. He was an old Shepherd dog, I'll never forget.

I thought, "Lord, this dog got more sense than a person."

When Grandmama got ready to milk cows, she could send that
dog up in the pasture and that dog would go up there...

And this is the truth,

He wouldn't bring nobody's cows down but Grandmama's.
That dog had just that much sense.

He would get around every one of them cows and bring them for milking.

When people hear me say that, a lot of them didn't believe it. They don't
believe you can train a dog like that. The dog name was "Old Bruce."

My Cousins

My Brother was the youngest in the group but he was the
biggest. He could whip them all except for one.

Now, He couldn't whip her. She could "hit hard as a man."

She'd put up her fist and tell him, "You ain't going to beat on me."

And give him a boom!"

She wasn't scared to "run into him."

Yes, she would. She was something else.

My Brother would make them fight. And if you
lost the fight, He'd whip you for losing.

Standing on My Own

My Daddy never co-signed for a bill for me. Every since I
was fourteen (14), He has let me go out and work.

I would buy my own clothes. Of course, I had to
give Papa some of the money, you know.

Money wasn't like it is now. When you got hold of fifty-cent,
you had some money. It would go a long way though.

Once I went down to the man that Daddy was dealing with. He had a pair
of shoes and hat that I liked. I told him, "I want them shoes and hat, will
you let me have them?" He said, "Did your Daddy tell you to get them?"

I didn't tell him a lie, I said, "No!"

He just looked at me. He said, "I'm going to let you have them
shoes and hat." He asked, "When are you going to pay me?"

I told him, "My Daddy would let me work it out
and I'd get paid off on the weekend."

I told him, I would pay him that Saturday. So, when
I got paid off, I went down and paid him.

From then on, I could go there and get "common things."

Nothing expensive!

I could get what I wanted and He'd let me have it.

I'd just go down and pay him, like I told him.

Nower days, Children are in a good thing. Daddies and Mamas
are paying bills for them. They don't know how good they
got it. Money wasn't circulating like that back then.

When I went into service...

My Grandfather gave me fifty-cent. I thought He had given me something big.

I have worked in my life time

from sun up, to sun down for fifty-cent a day...a "whole day."

I thought I had made something.

I remember when, me and my "whole family" would go out
and chop cotton and you know how much we made?

We made two-dollars and fifty-cent, for that day...all of us together.

But that was some money now.

You could buy a lot of grocery, honey.

You could buy a sack of flour, sugar, and coffee. You could get by on meal
and lard. You didn't have to buy nothing like that because we raised that.

Meal, meat, chicken, lard, vegetables, eggs and butter such as that we had.

I remember one year...

Mama had over five-hundred chickens on the yard. She kept five or six
in the coop all the time. When she got ready for a chicken, she would put
them up for killing. She'd feed them corn and chicken feed, you know!

Well, tell the truth,

Even when me' and your Mama was married, we had over one-hundred
and something chickens on the yard. We had three good milk cows.

I would milk two of them and carry the milk in the house. One of the cows,
I just poured the milk in the hog croft because we'd get so much milk.

I had all those chickens and I had made my mind up that I would sell some

chickens and butter.

We had just all kind of butter stacked up. Your Mama had a little mold "trick" that she made the butter up in round cakes, like you see in the stores now.

I went around asking people did they want butter and chicken? Everybody said, "Yeah, Yeah, bring it!"

When I went with the load, you know,

I sold "no butter" and "gave away" one chicken.

When I got back to the house, I said, "I ain't going back out with this no more!" Now, you see they don't want this.

They wanted it but they wanted it on credit. But your Mama didn't tell me to sell it on credit.

The Month of August

My Mama would get us ready for winter's canning. There were
a lot of things going on in the winter months. She would can
a lot of fruits through August. Also, in August we would pick
cotton. We also had Revival in the month of August.

We would pick cotton a certain length of time in the day, and go
to church; come back after service that day, go back to the field
and pick until dark. Then, that night, go "back to church."

See, People don't go to church in the daytime now, like they did then.

We had to go to Church, whether we wanted to or not.
They didn't allow us to "have our own way."

We had to do according to what Mama and Papa said and it didn't
make no difference how old we got. We still had to obey.

You didn't get grown as long as you were in their house.
You "had" to to what they said or else!

We were "very careful" what we said to our Parents. We were
not allowed to talk back at them. We "knew better!"

They didn't have any problems raising Children. We didn't have
any problems either, arguing with one another, as siblings.

They didn't allow us to do that. In fact, we were very crazy about one another.

You take my Brother, He was the oldest...

I could just do him "any kind of way." He would just
put up with what I would do to him.

We would get out there sometimes and just play so rough.
Mama would have to talk about whipping us.

I would scuffle with him. I couldn't handle him because he was much bigger
than I was. I was pretty fast though. I could throw him but I couldn't hold him.

I Stole Your Mother

They didn't give "away" girls, in marriage back then, like they do today. Parents were very skeptical about giving their daughters to boys.

So, when my cousin went to get his wife, asking for her hand in marriage, Her Mother told Him, "Oh, I'd rather give you one of my husband big old fine mules, than to give you my daughter!"

They joked a long time about that.

Your Mother stayed with her Grandparents. Her Grandma didn't
want me to marry her. That's why I married her, when I did.

I went over there one Sunday, and her Grandma almost knocked me out of the chair. She didn't want me there. Your Mother was almost crying when I left there.

My Brother-in-Law was the one who really went there and got her. I had
already gotten my Marriage License about a week or two before.

She and her Cousin came over to the store. I would go over
to the store a lot of the times, just hanging out.

The next morning, they came again. I started to take her then and go ahead
and marry her. Her cousin said, "No! Because she knew they would blame her.

There was another time I wanted to get her, but I "walked up on"
her Brother and Uncle, so, I had to leave her that day too.

I told her, "I'm going to send over there for you, and you come
out!" I said,"Now, you be sure, when you come out, don't
hesitate!" and she didn't. She came out running!!!

A cousin of mine carried us to the Preacher's house and that's
where we were married. I forgot the Preacher's name.

They didn't like it and they got mad, but I got them "straight."

I told her Cousin, "You better be trying to get you somebody too."

I wasn't trying to "run over her." I was trying to get me somebody to stay with.

They didn't like it for about a week.

Your Mother didn't go back to her house for about a week, and to my
surprise; her Grandma came back with her. She had kind of calm down.

Me And Your Mother

I remember one Christmas, I'd been out. I had gotten some of that "bad stuff" in me. I came home late that night.

We "bought" Christmas for the Children.

I had a bag of apples, bananas, oranges trying to get them out of the car. And by me being "full of that bad stuff"...

I was dropping apples, bananas, and oranges everywhere.

I didn't know it then...

The Children got up the next morning and they really enjoyed Christmas.

They went outside...

They saw fruits down by where I had parked the car.

The Children was running, picking them up, saying, "Look! Look! This is the way Santa Claus came."

"See, This is where He came right here!"

Me and your Mama was just killing ourselves laughing. We were tickled to death at the Children. It was so funny.

It really made me feel good to see the Children enjoy Christmas.

We later got our own house...

We had a house built, just before Christmas.

The morning of the moving, My Cousin and I went to sell cotton. I didn't know it, but when I got back; I drove up to the house and the house was empty.

I said, "Looka' here!"

I knew what had happened though.

So, I just went on down to the new house. Your Mother had moved "everything." We had Christmas there. That was a happy day. I will never forget that.

Raising Children

We had some difficulties but it was good. A lot of things, I disagreed with. Especially, when it came to y'all Children.

I was very particular with y'all...very particular.

I didn't want y'all to get hurt no kind of way...or nothing like that.

I was particular about where y'all go...and who y'all were with.

Your Mama wanted your Sister to go to School in Jackson. I made a mistake there. I should of let her went to school. But I was afraid that they weren't going to treat her right.

I said, "No, I'm not doing it." I said, "I'm going to get in some trouble, so the best thing for me to do was to not let her go." And I didn't but I should have. Yes, I should have.

I see she would have been real smart.

I see I made a mistake there. But I was just that particular.

It was not that I thought my Children was better than other folks, but I just didn't allow anybody to mess with y'all.

One day,

the man I rented land from, came up to the house.

See, He would go out and pick up workers and carry them to the field.

Now, when I started working with Him, I told Him how I was. I said, "My Wife and Children, now, I don't allow "NOBODY" to mess with them."

I said, "If you want me to do anything, you just ask me and if it's anyway possible;

I'll do it."

So, one morning up there...

And, I was drinking at that particular time.

He came up there...

Some of the Children said, "Daddy, Mr. 'Man' out there."

I had just drove up, after being out all night. It was cold and...

I was about to get out again.

So, with my shirt down to my waist, and with that bad
whiskey in me, I walked out there in the cold...

He started to go off, about what I need to do, about "this" and "that."

I said, "Now, Hold on!"

I said, "Now, I didn't buy your place but...

you have come up here in the wrong way."

"Now, as long as I'm up here, I'm going to be the boss on this hill."

"This is your place alright enough but you got to come up here right!"

He left there and I was never again worried with him. They
said me and him wouldn't get along but I made more money
with him than any man I ever lived on land with.

I did!

I never had anymore trouble with him. That was the first time and last time.

I guess, He seen I wasn't going to take it.

I'm sure somebody had told him how I was. I was "hot-tempered." I would have fought him, I would have.

Tell the truth,

I was a good man BUT, I didn't take nothing off people and people "pretty much" knew that.

I mean, I treated everybody right...

If people saw me coming, they knew they was going to get "something funny" out of me. They knew I was always joking or "carrying on!"

I never was' a scrapper.

Well, only with one person and I was so bad wrong.

Yeah, but other than that; I always tried to carry myself in a way that I could go

"through the world."

Go Home!

My two oldest boys had started going out.

The oldest one would come home before night and do his chores.

something told me, "It's time for you to go to the house."

"You are going to find that boy "out there" and you're going
to try and tell him, "you need to be at home" and the boy can
tell you, "you're the one who need to be at home!"

I remember,

On evening I had been back up in the hills and I had taken a drink with a
friend of mine. I started home and ran in a ditch and couldn't get out.

A Cousin of mine lived across the road, so I went up and got him. He carried
me to my Brother-in Law's house. He came and pulled me out the ditch.

It was daylight when I got home.

Your Mama was getting out of the bed and I got in the
bed. That was the last time I'd taken a drink.

I had already been converted!

I was in the fields and "something" just whipped me
and said, "It's time for you to be at home!"

I had a half of carton of cigarettes and almost a can of Prince
Albert tobacco. I quit smoking right then and quit chewing
tobacco. Neither one of them bothered me to quit.

I never will forget it!

When I decided to quit drinking, two of my Cousins took me
out. They thought I didn't know where they were going.

I knew "EXACTLY" what they were up to.

They said, "Ahh, come on and go with us! I said, "Alright."

We got over to where they were going, and sat
down. They got their beer, you know!

They said, "Take one!

I said, "No, I've made up my mind and I'm going to serve the Lord!"

They said, "Man, take one!"

See, they knew how I was before...with them.

It was like that, when I use to beg them, you know!

I said, "No, Y'all just go ahead! So, they went on that time.

The next time they came at me, they had made up in their
mind that they would get me to drink, this time.

They said, "Come on and go with us "fellow!"

"We ain't going to be gone long." So, I went with them.

I first told them NO, because I knew where they was going.

So, sure enough, we went on to that same place. They sit down and went to
drinking and asking me "again." I said, "No, I just ain't going to drink!"

They never bothered me again. They didn't come to get me anymore either.

I had made up in my mind to serve the Lord, Now that's what I'm going to do!

I later joined the Church and was trained on what to do in Church.

I was put on trial as a Deacon and still serve as a Deacon today.

[This book has been rewritten, so I add...My Daddy
served faithfully until his death]

In the Army Now

IN 1943, I believe it was at Camp Shelby that I was enlisted. We returned home. I stayed about three weeks. Then, I called to Fort Bennett Georgia. That's where we took our Basic Training.

I stayed there about six months in Georgia, then I left and went to Kentucky and we stayed there I guess, around nine months. Afterwards, we left Kentucky, went over-seas and stayed there "ever-so-long."

We were transferring back and forth to France, then to Germany. We would haul a load of gas, ammunition, or food; whatever they needed up there on the front.

We had to bring a load of prisoners back every trip. On one of our trips, I was coming back, a German Solider came out on the highway with his hands up and just gave himself up. I started to run over him because I didn't know what he was up to.

I was on the tail-end, which I wasn't "supposed to be." I had broken rank. I was supposed to be the seventh truck but I "fooled-around" and got on the tail-end of the convoy that day.

I got out and put my gun on him and made him get in the back with the rest of the prisoners. I didn't get any credit for that German capture. I didn't get any credit for none of that,

you see!

My records don't show that. If I had known like I know now, I would have had all of that written down. Many of them, like our Sergeants, and Platoon Sergeants; they were writing "such as that down." I didn't understand to do that. I was saying, "All forget it!" I was young, I was only about nineteen.

When we went over to Germany,

going over, it was really rough. We stayed on the water twenty-seven days
and nights. Some days we would anchor down out there, probably a week,
not leaving there and "couldn't sometimes" come up on top deck.

Of course, coming back, we didn't have that kind of trouble.
We weren't but seven days coming back over.

I really asked the Lord to take me because I didn't have any joy. But
the Lord seen I wasn't "fit" to go. He let me know, "It's my water, this
is my ocean and I govern the waters, just like I do the land."

We had some good and bad Sergeants.

We had one in Georgia, He was rotten. He would tell you, "If my
Momma is in that barrack and I say, fall out on the double, she
better come out of there!" And he wouldn't be joking either.

He would say, "If she tears the door down, I'll have them to put it back up!"

If you didn't do what He said, He would put you out on a hill, digging a six-
by-six, where all those rocks were and; when you finished digging, He'd throw
a cigarette butt or a match stem in there and tell you to cover it back up.

He was terrible!

But now, the Sergeant that went overseas with us;
You couldn't beat a better Sergeant.

He told a couple of Commanders, "Now, my men here, they
are Soldiers, they are "with us." He kept our backs!

Sometimes, He would tell them to give us a pass. He would say,
"If they want to go up town, let them go!" "If they are not back,
I'll know what to do for them; and He did." He would punish
you for sure if you didn't do what you were supposed to do.

If you weren't back at the Camp at a certain time, He'd put you on
extra duty. But, if you "were back" you'd get a pass every time.

He was a real good Sergeant.

I went through a whole lot. It was a lot of danger.
I came very close to getting killed

one time.

Once I was in my fox-hole and I wasn't down low enough and when that
hand-grenade busted; It's a slug that came off that hand-grenade,

just right over my head. If it had hit me,

it probably would have killed me.

That's one reason I said the Lord blessed me to go and come back safe. The Lord
gave me consolation and understanding, that HE HAD THE POWER! You can
go into a lot of dangerous places and HE WILL CARRY YOU THROUGH.

When we came off that field, that's where I got my
furlough, and I came home that same evening.

Three Generations of Service

I was sitting and talking with my Father about World War II. He shared with me, many interesting stories. I thought they were good stories, and I began to ask other questions. These are some of the questions that I asked and some of the comments he made.

What year did you go? In 1943, I believe it was. It was at Camp Shelby. That is where I was enlisted at. We returned back home, and I stayed about three weeks and was called to Georgia. That was where we took our basic training at Fort Bennett Georgia.

What happened when you came back home? I stayed a couple of years single, and then I married your Mama. I started back farming. I worked out on the dam. I worked out there for about a year and a half, I imagine, and then I believe I started back to farming again.

How did you feel about your daughter going to the Army? I really didn't object to it, BUT, I didn't want her to go; knowing what I had been through. I didn't want my daughter to be in that kind of danger. I wasn't nervous, but I wasn't pleased. I didn't agree, but I didn't kick on it. She went and the Lord brought her back.

Your Mama and I didn't really agree together on that. I reckon she saw that She was going to go, and I guess she thought that was alright. She had to sign for her, because she was quite young when she went into the Service.

How did you feel about the Grandchildren going? I didn't kick on them so bad, because they had made up their minds to go, and their mother had too. I tried to tell them, to the best of my knowledge, what I had to go through. It's a lot different though.

There's a lot of dust over there where they were. We didn't have such as that, but we had water and mud when we were taking our basic training.

How I felt when writing this story?

Writing this story, as well as the story of my Daddy has been a great honor. So many things I "assumed" about him. Talking to him, I find that all of these thoughts, that I had in my head as a child was of Satan. He is such a deciever.

If you are reading this book and you "feel" that your Daddy
(or any other family member) do not love you, please go and
sit down and talk to them. DO NOT ASSUME!

My Father and Mother were great parents. I'm grateful to God for loaning them to me. They may not have given me what I "thought" I wanted

but they surely gave me what I NEEDED!

I PRAISE YOU JESUS!!!

Author's Biography

I am Evangelist Doris C. Smith. I am a Pastor & License Kingdom Life Coach.

I am a 1980 Graduate of Grenada High School.

I have an Associate Degree in Childhood Development.

I have a Certificate from National Christian Counselor Association.

A Bachelor of Arts in Christian Psychology, International College of Ministry.

Also, Certificate of Ordination & Ministry License.

Certificate of Achievement, From Darkness to Light.

Certified Temperament Counselor; Sarasota, Florida.

Certification of Training; Overcoming Abuse God's Way.

A.M.E.N. Ministries; Life Coaching/Mentoring

My Biggest Accomplishment is:

Being Born Again: November 4, 1991

Accepted Call in the Ministry: October 9, 1999

Contact Information

E-mail Address: dorissmith217@yahoo.com

P. O. Box 174 Grenada, MS 38901

Phone Number: 662-614-3402